DIFFERENT DOGS

ALVIN SILVERSTEIN · VIRGINIA SILVERSTEIN · LAURA SILVERSTEIN NUNN

TWENTY-FIRST CENTURY BOOKS
BROOKFIELD, CONNECTICUT

Cover photograph courtesy of Animals Animals (© Charles Palek)

Photographs courtesy of Animals Animals: pp. 6 (© Robert Pearcy), 10 (© Ralph Reinhold),
14 (© Zig Leszczynski), 22 (© Robert Pearcy), 30 (© Robert Pearcy), 34 (©Ralph Reinhold),
38 (© Robert Pearcy), 42 (© Mickey Gibson); © Norvia Behling: pp. 18, 26

Cover Design by Karen Quigley
Interior Design by Claire Fontaine

Library of Congress Cataloging-in-Publication Data
Silverstein, Alvin.
Different dogs/Alvin Silverstein, Virginia Silverstein, Laura Silverstein Nunn.
p. cm. — (What a pet!)
Includes bibliographical references and Index.
Summary: Examines the pros and cons of keeping less common dog breeds such as akitas, chihuahuas,
and Saint Bernards, discussing their care, feeding, and emotional needs.

ISBN 0-7613-1371-0 (lib. bdg.)
1. Dog breeds—Juvenile literature. [1. Dog breeds. 2. Dogs.] I. Silverstein, Virginia B. II. Nunn, Laura
Silverstein. III. Title. IV. Series: Silverstein, Alvin. What a pet!

SF426.5.S535   2000
636.7—dc21
                                                                                            98-52109
                                                                                            CIP
                                                                                            AC

Published by Twenty-First Century Books
A Division of The Millbrook Press, Inc.
2 Old New Milford Road
Brookfield, CT 06804

Visit us at our Web site: www.millbrookpress.com

CONTENTS

THE DOG BREEDS

The American Kennel Club classifies the dog breeds in groups:

- Sporting: spaniels, retrievers, setters, and pointers
- Hound: hunting dogs, including basenjis, dachshunds, and greyhounds
- Working: dogs bred for guarding, hunting, and other jobs—including Akitas and Saint Bernards
- Terrier: feisty dogs bred to kill vermin
- Toy: small dogs, including Chihuahuas and shih tzus
- Non-Sporting: a varied group including bulldogs and shar-peis
- Herding: working dogs that herd other animals, including corgis

These groupings are rather arbitrary—why, for instance, is a dachshund a hound and not a terrier?—and other dog clubs use somewhat different classifications. Psychologist Stanley Coren suggests that pets could be better matched to owners if they were grouped by type of behavior:

- Friendly dogs: including cocker spaniels, collies, and retrievers
- Protective dogs: including Akitas, boxers, chows, and rottweilers
- Independent dogs: including dalmatians, greyhounds, and shar-peis
- Self-assured dogs: including basenjis, shih tzus, and terriers
- Consistent dogs: including Chihuahuas, dachshunds, and Pekingese
- Steady dogs: including bulldogs, Great Danes, and Saint Bernards
- Clever dogs: including border collies, corgis, and poodles

WHAT A PET!

THIS SERIES WILL GIVE you information about some well-known animals and some unusual ones. It will help you to select a pet suitable for your family and for where you live. It will also tell you about animals that should *not* be pets. It is important for you to understand that many people who work with animals are strongly opposed to keeping *any* wild creature as a pet.

People tend to want to keep exotic animals. But they forget that often it is illegal to have them as pets, or that they require a great deal of special care and will never really become good pets. A current fad of owning an exotic animal may quickly pass, and the animals suffer. Their owners may abandon them in an effort to return them to the wild, even though the animals can no longer survive there. Or they may languish in small cages without proper food and exercise.

Before selecting any animal as a pet, it is a good idea to learn as much as you can about it. This series will help you, and your local veterinarian and the ASPCA are good sources of information. You should also find out if it is endangered. Phone numbers for each state wildlife agency can be found on the Internet at

http://www.animalsforsale.com/states.htm

and you can get an updated list of endangered and threatened species on the Internet at

http://jjwww.fws.gov/r9endspp/endspp.html "Endangered Species Home Page, U.S. Fish & Wildlife Service"

Any pet is a big responsibility—*your* responsibility. The most important thing to keep in mind when selecting a pet is the welfare of the animal.

FAST FACTS

Scientific name	*Canis familaris* in Family Canidae, Order Carnivora
Cost	Up to $1,000 for show quality
Food	Commercial dog food
Housing	Can be kept indoors freely if properly trained; or may be kept in a wire mesh cage or in an outdoor kennel. Outdoors, dog needs shelter. Indoors, dog needs a bed (or crate) and should have chew toys.
Training	Needs a lot of patience for training. Dog treats are very effective for tricks. Can housebreak using a crate, or paper train; should learn to wear collar and leash; can learn basic commands, such as "Sit," "Come," "Stay," "Heel," and "No." Can also learn tricks such as rolling over, playing dead, fetch, carry newspaper.
Special notes	Before getting an Akita puppy, check with the breeder to make sure its parents do not have hereditary health problems such as abnormal hip structure (dysplasia) or eye problems.

AKITA

DOG-LOVERS ALL OVER Japan know the story of Hachiko, an Akita whose love and loyalty warmed the hearts of an entire nation. Hachiko lived with Professor Eisaburo Ueno, who taught at Tokyo Imperial University. Every morning, Hachiko walked with his owner to the nearby train station to see him off to work. Every evening, the dog met the professor at the train station and they walked home together.

One evening in 1925, Hachiko waited for his master at the train station as usual, but the professor never returned. He had died from a stroke at the university. Hachiko was sent to live with the professor's relatives several miles away. But every evening, the faithful Akita went to the train station to wait for his beloved professor. After the train arrived, he would walk back home alone. Hachiko continued to do this for the next nine years until his death in 1934.

DID YOU KNOW?
The Akita has been declared a national monument and national treasure in its native country of Japan.

Our First Friends

Dogs were the first animals to be domesticated by humans. Scientists believe that dogs first began to live with people as long as 12,000 to 14,000 years ago, when humans were hunters and gatherers. Wild dogs were drawn to the garbage dumps near the camps and soon got used to this easy source of food. People started to tame the dogs, and the animals became very important to them. Dogs kept the campsites clean by eating garbage, and they barked to warn the people of approaching strangers.

After these dogs were tamed, people started to breed them for specific physical traits—such as size, shape, and colors—and abilities, such as the ability to guard or hunt. Eventually, specific breeds were developed. Today, the American Kennel Club recognizes more than 140 different breeds of dogs, but there are hundreds more distinct breeds around the world.

Hachiko became a living legend. A bronze statue of him was placed in the train station as a symbol of loyalty. It was dogs like Hachiko who inspired the famous saying, "A dog is man's best friend."

THE ORIGIN OF THE AKITA

Akitas belong to one of the most ancient types of dogs, the spitz group, which are very similar to their wolflike ancestors. *Spitz* means "pointed," referring to the shape of their muzzle. These sturdy dogs typically have upstanding ears, an up-curling tail, and thick fur that helps them keep warm in the northern lands where they originated.

It is thought that invaders from Korea first brought dogs similar to today's Akitas to Japan around 8000 B.C. People in the mountains of northern Japan began to use them as hunting dogs. During the twelfth and thirteenth centuries, warrior knights (Samurai) used Akita-like dogs for the sport of dog fighting. Later, they were bred as guard dogs, hunting dogs, and herding dogs. In the early seventeenth century, breeders in the Akita district selected the best of the hunting dogs to produce a breed so elite that only the ruling family and aristocrats of Japan were allowed to own them. The nineteenth century brought many changes to Japan, as industrialization and contacts with traders from the West caused many people to move to cities. Akitas began to be used as family guardians. They were also crossbred with mastiffs, Great Danes, Saint Bernards, and bulldogs, as well as with the tosa, a powerful Japanese fighting dog. The new crossbreeds were called "shin-akita" (improved dogs) and were the ancestors of the American Akita breed.

> **DID YOU KNOW?**
> Bred as hunting dogs, Akitas hunted down bears, boars, and other large game. The dog would corner its prey and then bark until its master came to make the kill.

Helen Keller was the first person to introduce Akitas into the United States, bringing home an Akita puppy from a visit to northern Japan in 1937. The breed did not catch on in the United States, however, until after World War II, when U.S. soldiers smuggled pet dogs back with them after finishing their service in

A Sacred Dog

The Akita has a spiritual importance to the Japanese people. Its image was carved on the tombs of ancient Japanese royalty. Today's Japanese regard the Akita as a symbol of good health. A typical gift for a newborn baby is a small statue of an Akita to symbolize health, happiness, and a long life. The statues are also sent as get-well presents when someone is ill.

Japan. The Akita's popularity got another boost when it was added to the American Kennel Club registry in 1973.

AKITAS AS PETS

The Akita looks like a bear, with a large, strong, bearlike head. Akitas are large dogs. Males are 26 to 28 inches (66 to 71 centimeters) tall at the shoulders and weigh an average 95 to 110 pounds (43 to 50 kilograms). Females are 24 to 26 inches (61 to 66 centimeters) tall and weigh 75 to 90 pounds (34 to 41 kilograms). Despite their large size, Akitas are very adaptable animals and can live comfortably in apartments.

The Akita's distinctive tail curls and lies on the animal's back. Akitas come in all sorts of colors and patterns. All, except white ones, have a distinct face mask. Like other northern dogs, the Akita has a very thick coat with two layers; the top layer is thick and coarse and the undercoat is thick and soft. The Akita sheds its coat twice each year. The insulating coat helps to protect it from both cold and hot weather.

Like their ancestors, today's Akitas make great guard dogs. They are very protective of their human family and are usually very wary of strangers. These dogs do not usually bark without reason, so when an Akita barks, pay attention. Akitas are very territorial and can be aggressive toward other dogs. Some experts say that Akitas may also become aggressive toward small children. But if the dog is raised around children and is properly trained, it will protect the children of the family—though not the neighbors' kids.

Akitas are highly intelligent. They can learn to obey various commands and perform tricks, but they get bored easily and may refuse to do what you ask. They are strong-willed dogs, and if they don't want to do something, they won't. Akitas are very affectionate animals, but they need a lot of love and patience during training. They have a life span of 10 to 14 years.

INTERNET RESOURCES

http://w3.mgr.com/mgr/howell/bobpages/breeds/akita.htm "Akita"

http://www.canismajor.com/dog/akita.html "The Akita: Loyal Friend from the Land of the Rising Sun," by Paula Ebner

http://www.media-akita.or.jp/akita-inu/akitas-topicsE.html "Akita-Inu Home Page"

http://www.nylana.org/RRACI/history.htm "Raritan River Akita Club Inc. Akita History Page," by Louis A. Fallon

http://www.oklahoma.net/~goldeagl/akita/akitfact.htm "Facts About Akitas"

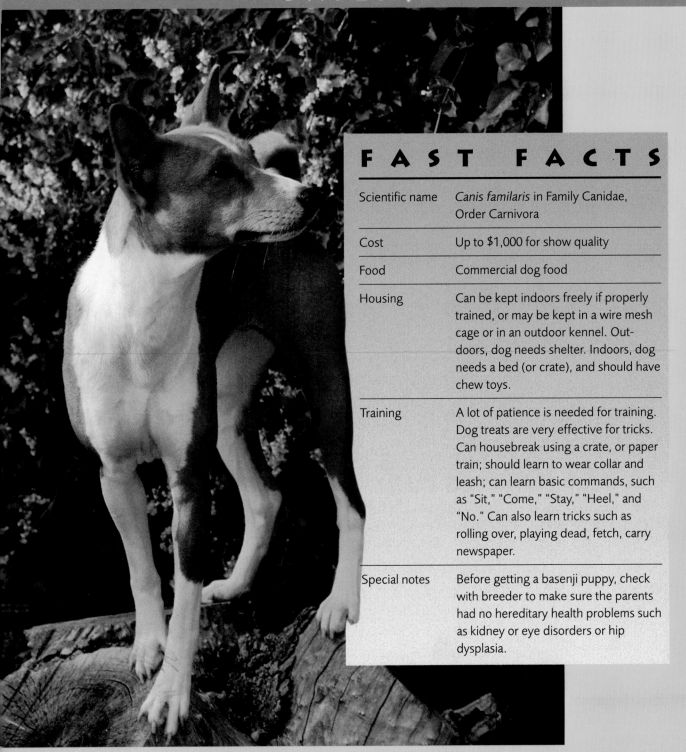

BASENJI

FAST FACTS

Scientific name	*Canis familaris* in Family Canidae, Order Carnivora
Cost	Up to $1,000 for show quality
Food	Commercial dog food
Housing	Can be kept indoors freely if properly trained, or may be kept in a wire mesh cage or in an outdoor kennel. Outdoors, dog needs shelter. Indoors, dog needs a bed (or crate), and should have chew toys.
Training	A lot of patience is needed for training. Dog treats are very effective for tricks. Can housebreak using a crate, or paper train; should learn to wear collar and leash; can learn basic commands, such as "Sit," "Come," "Stay," "Heel," and "No." Can also learn tricks such as rolling over, playing dead, fetch, carry newspaper.
Special notes	Before getting a basenji puppy, check with breeder to make sure the parents had no hereditary health problems such as kidney or eye disorders or hip dysplasia.

BASENJI

BARKING DOGS CAN be really annoying. But would you believe that there is a breed of dog that doesn't bark? The basenji, an African dog, is nicknamed the "barkless dog." One reason why the basenji doesn't bark may be the different structure of its voice box, compared to that of other dogs. Actually, basenjis can bark but usually do not (or bark only once). But they do make a variety of other sounds—they growl, whine, yip, and howl. They are also known for the "yodel" sound that they make when they are happy. Though basenjis are generally known for being quiet, some can be rather noisy, especially when they are left alone.

Many pet owners say that basenjis are elegant-looking dogs that are lovable, playful, and fairly quiet. But they can be quite a challenge. Given love, patience, and proper training, the basenji can make a great pet.

THE ORIGIN OF THE BASENJI

The basenji is one of the oldest dog breeds; its origin dates back to around 5000 B.C. These first dogs were brought down the Nile as presents from the people of Central Africa to the pharaohs of ancient Egypt. Basenjis became palace dogs and were depicted in Egyptian engravings and sculptures as hunting dogs and as valued house pets lying under the pharaoh's chair. For thousands of years, basenjis lived among the people of ancient Egypt. But when the ancient Egyptian civilization declined and fell, the basenjis in Egypt disappeared without a trace.

It was not until the late 1800s that the basenji was rediscovered in its native land of Central Africa. In 1870, British explorers described the basenji dogs they encountered during a visit to Africa. In 1895 the first pair of basenjis was brought to England by British explorers. These dogs, however, died from distemper a short time later. Efforts to bring more basenjis into Europe were not successful until 1936, when Mrs. Olivia Burns imported a pair of basenjis into England. The following year, the first basenji puppies were born in England. At the same time,

> ## A Dog's Senses
>
> *The basenji, like all other dogs, has amazing senses, many of which are far better than those of humans.*
>
> *A dog's sense of smell is definitely its most powerful sense—a million times more sensitive than ours. A dog can follow a trail that is weeks old and even trace a person's scent under water.*
>
> *Dogs have remarkable hearing. They can hear about four times better than humans. They can also hear high-pitched sounds that we cannot hear.*
>
> *Dogs can notice movement at a greater distance than we can, but they cannot see as well up close. They can see better than we can in the dark, but they see things in shades of black and white, not in color.*
>
> *Dogs have fewer taste buds than we do. That's why they are likely to eat just about anything—and they usually do. So beware of what your dog eats. Never give a dog chocolate, which can poison it, and don't let it lap up antifreeze, which has a sweet taste.*

a pair of basenjis was brought to America by Mrs. Byron Rogers of New York City. Unfortunately, this pair and their litter died from distemper. Basenji puppies were first born and raised successfully in America in 1941.

The basenji was added to the American Kennel Club registry in 1943.

BASENJIS AS PETS

The basenji is an elegant, graceful dog that moves swiftly and is often compared to a little deer. The male basenji is an average of 17 inches (43 centimeters) tall at the shoulder and weighs about 24 pounds (11 kilograms); the female is about 16 inches (41 centimeters) at the shoulder and about 22 pounds (10 kilograms).

The basenji is admired for its attractive short, silky coat. The coat's color may be brownish red, red, black, or tricolor (with white), with various markings. This breed also has an unmistakable tight curly tail that rests on the dog's backside.

DID YOU KNOW?
Basenjis do not like to go outside when it's raining. They really don't like to get wet. So don't try to give a basenji a bath—it won't be any fun for anybody.

Basenjis are very clean animals. They clean themselves much the way a cat does. If a basenji gets muddy, it won't be that way for long.

Basenjis are very active and playful dogs. They usually get along very well with children and love their owners. But they may be cautious with strangers.

Basenjis are smart, but they are also quite independent. So, while they are capable of being trained and can learn to do tricks, they may simply refuse to obey just because they don't want to. They must be properly trained, however, because a basenji can be very mischievous and will do a lot of damage if it is not corrected.

A healthy, properly cared for basenji will live for 10 to 13 years.

INTERNET RESOURCES

http://basenji.nre.com/basenji.html "Out of Africa, into Your Heart," by Don Worsham

http://w3.mgr.com/mgr/howell/bobpages/breeds/basenji.htm "Basenji"

http://www.aic.net.au/~hunts/basinfo.htm "Basenji Breed Information," by the Basenji Club of New South Wales

http://www.barkless.com/ebc/intro.htm "An Introduction to the Basenji," by the Evergreen Basenji Club

http://www.bright.net/~rstack/dogs/Basenji.HTM "Basenji"

http://www.canismajor.com/dog/basenji.html "The Basenji: Ancient African Breed Rediscovered," by Tracy A. Leonard, DVM

http://www.k9web.com/dog-faqs/breeds/basenjis.html "Basenjis," by Elizabeth Adams, Ann Potter, Troy Shadbolt, and Fred Sienko (a very thorough FAQ)

http://www.nobark.com/whatis.htm "What Is a Basenji?"

BULLDOG

FAST FACTS

Scientific name	*Canis familaris* in Family Canidae, Order Carnivora
Cost	May range from $800 to $1500
Food	Commercial dog food
Housing	Can be kept indoors freely if properly trained, or may be kept in a wire mesh cage or in an outdoor kennel. Outdoors, dog needs shelter. Indoors, dog needs a bed (or crate), and should have chew toys.
Training	A lot of patience needed for training. Dog treats are very effective for tricks. Can housebreak using a crate, or paper train; should learn to wear collar and leash; can learn basic commands, such as "Sit," "Come," "Stay," "Heel," and "No." May also learn tricks such as rolling over, playing dead, fetching, carrying newspaper.
Special notes	May suffer from hip and knee problems, heart disease, tail infections, eye inflammation, and breathing problems. May get heat stroke if in the heat for too long.

BULLDOG

LOOKS CAN BE DECEIVING. Some people think that bulldogs look tough, mean, and even frightening. That may have been true a few centuries ago, when bulldogs were indeed vicious. Today's bulldogs, however, are actually one of the friendliest dog breeds; they are sweet and affectionate, and they love people.

Bulldogs Are Not Pit Bulls

Some people confuse a bulldog and a pit bull, but the breeds are quite different. The pit bull was developed in nineteenth-century England, bred from bulldogs and terriers. Pit bulls were used as fighting dogs, but unlike today's sweet-natured bulldogs, most pit bulls have kept their vicious traits. Some are kept by drug dealers and other criminals, to protect them from their enemies and frighten their victims. Pit bulls are involved in so many dog-bite incidents that some communities ban the breed.

THE ORIGIN OF THE BULLDOG

The bulldog, also called English bulldog, has been around since the early thirteenth century, when bullbaiting was a popular sport in England. Several dogs were set loose on a bull in a ring or in a village square. The dogs would grab the bull by the nose and hang on at all costs. The attacks of the dogs angered the bull, who tried to shake them loose and injure or kill them. These fights were brutal. The bulldog, bred from mastiff and terrier stock, got its name from the bullbaiting sport. Bulldogs were known for being powerful, courageous, and stubborn. Bullbaiting was not only a popular sport but also useful for butchers, who believed that the dogs tenderized beef by draining the blood out of the bull.

In 1835 bullbaiting was outlawed. Bulldogs lost their usefulness, and soon few of them were left. Bulldog lovers saved the breed by turning this deadly fighter into a good-natured companion. They kept its broad, heavy body and typical bulldog face, but bred out the viciousness. Today's bulldog is mild-mannered and affectionate, but it is still physically tough, with a built-in instinct for holding on tight, no matter what. (You can test this trait by playing tug-of-war with a bulldog using a piece of rope.)

Bulldog Breeds

Unlike the English bulldog, the American bulldog is not registered with the American Kennel Club. American bulldogs are bred for their working qualities, not for show, like the AKC breeds. They are strong, sturdy dogs, not as prone to health problems as English bulldogs, and they are often kept as guard dogs. (Like other bulldogs, they bite to hold on, not to injure.) Owners can show off their dogs' working skills at shows sponsored by the American Bulldog Association.

The French bulldog, often called the "Frenchie," is a smaller version of the English bulldog, weighing an average of 25 to 30 pounds (11 to 14 kilograms). The French bulldog was bred from toy bulldogs sent over to France from England in the late nineteenth century. The breed is registered with the American Kennel Club. These small dogs are kept as pets and show dogs, rather than as working dogs.

BULLDOGS AS PETS

The bulldog is a rather short, stocky dog, about 13 to 15 inches (34 to 38 centimeters) tall at the shoulders. But they would not make good lap pets. How would you like to have a 40-pound (18-kilogram) female bulldog or a 50-pound (23-kilogram) male sitting on you? Bulldogs may be small in height, but they are pretty big in weight.

The bulldog has a large head, folded ears, a short muzzle, a protruding lower jaw, and loose skin that forms wrinkles on the head and face. Its short, fine coat is tan, white, reddish brown, or brindle (patches or streaks of color, such as red, brown, or gray).

Bulldogs' stocky build and short legs make them very slow-moving animals with a low activity level. But that doesn't mean that bulldogs can't play with children. In fact, bulldogs are usually good with children.

Bulldogs make good guard dogs. They rarely bark for no reason, but if they feel threatened, they will bark and latch onto the intruder with their teeth.

Bulldogs are intelligent, but they are very stubborn and may appear not too smart. If they don't want to do something, they won't. Training them takes a lot of patience.

Bulldogs are expensive because they have a lot of breeding problems. In fact, they are unable to give birth to their puppies on their own and have a high puppy death rate. Generally a veterinarian must deliver the puppies by surgery and treat the mother with hormones to help her accept the puppies.

The bulldog is a short-lived breed, with a life span of 8 to 10 years.

INTERNET RESOURCES

http://w3.mgr.com/mgr/howell/bobpages/breeds/bulldog.htm "Bulldog"

http://www.american-bulldog.com/a_peek.html "A Peek into Genuine Bulldog History. An excerpt from Dogs: Their History and Development (1927)," by Edward C. Ash

http://www.american-bulldog.com/about_the_ab.html "About the American Bulldog," by the American Bulldog Association

http://www.bulldog.org/bulldogs/ "The Bulldogs' Home Page"

http://www.frenchbulldog.org/faq.html "French Bulldogs" (FAQ), by Carol Gravestock-Taylor

http://www.io.com/~wilf/bulldog—1/faq.html "The Bulldog FAQ," by Wilf LeBlanc and others

FAST FACTS

Scientific name	*Canis familaris* in Family Canidae, Order Carnivora
Cost	About $200 and up
Food	Commercial dog food
Housing	Should be kept indoors. Can be kept in a crate or dog bed, and should have chew toys.
Training	A lot of patience needed for training. Dog treats are very effective for tricks. Can housebreak using a crate, or paper train, or litter train; should learn to wear collar and leash; can learn basic commands, such as "Sit," "Come," "Stay," "Heel," and "No." Can also learn tricks such as rolling over, playing dead, fetching.
Special notes	Before getting a Chihuahua, ask the breeder about any health problems in the parents, including knee and eye problems; have it checked for heart defects.

CHIHUAHUA

CHIHUAHUAS ARE GREAT traveling companions. They are so small that you could carry one around in your backpack or inside your jacket. Chihuahuas know when to be quiet, so no one would even know that you're hiding a tiny animal, especially a dog! But when it's time to make an appearance, the Chihuahua will bark to make its presence known.

Chihuahuas are devoted to their owners. They are extremely loyal and very protective of their masters. They are very affectionate dogs and love attention. Chihuahuas are easier to handle than larger dog breeds, but they need just as much care as any other pet.

> **DID YOU KNOW?**
> The Chihuahua, the smallest of all the dog breeds, is the only "natural" toy breed. It was not bred down from large dogs, as all the other toy breeds were.

THE ORIGIN OF THE CHIHUAHUA

The origin of the Chihuahua remains a mystery. But scientists do know that the Chihuahua is a very old breed, dating from as early as the ninth century. During this time, the ancient Toltecs, in what is now Mexico, made stone carvings of a small dog, the techichi. It was a long-haired dog that looked very much like today's Chihuahua but was somewhat larger. This ancient dog is believed to be the ancestor of the Chihuahua.

The techichi was used in Toltec religious ceremonies and was believed to have spiritual powers. When the Toltecs were conquered by the Aztecs, the techichi was prized by the conquerors, too. In the flourishing civilization built by the Aztecs, techichis became pampered pets of the rich. Blue-colored ones, in particular, were regarded as sacred. In 1520, however, the Aztecs were conquered by explorer Hernando Cortés and his crew. The Spaniards had little interest in the techichi, and it is believed that these little animals were left to survive in the wild.

It is not certain how the techichi developed into the modern Chihuahua. Breeders believe that the small Mexican dog was crossed with even smaller hairless dogs that had been brought to the Americas from Asia back in prehistoric times when a land bridge connected Siberia and Alaska. There are no records of the breed for several centuries after the Spanish conquest. In 1850, however, some very small dogs were found in some old ruins, thought to be the remains of the Aztec emperor Montezuma's palace. These dogs—some long-haired, some short-haired, and some hairless—were named after the Mexican state in which they were found, Chihuahua. The hairless variety became known as the Mexican hairless.

The Chihuahua was relatively unknown to the public until the early 1920s. Then Chihuahuas began to appear in the movies and on television with Xavier Cugat, a popular bandleader, and the tiny dog breed finally got widespread exposure. The Chihuahua was registered with the American Kennel Club in the early 1900s, but it was not until the 1960s that it became very popular all over the world.

CHIHUAHUAS AS PETS

Chihuahuas are the smallest dogs in the world, measuring about 6 to 9 inches (15 to 23 centimeters) tall at the shoulders and weighing less than 6 pounds (3 kilograms). The coat can be long or short, and can be various colors and solid, marked, or streaked.

Chihuahuas are great lapdogs. They are small and cuddly and very friendly. Chihuahuas form very strong bonds with their owners, often to one or two specific people. They even love to sleep with their owners at night and burrow under the covers. Chihuahuas are often wary of strangers and may greet them with a little nibble at the ankles. But Chihuahuas do not have to be yappy, ankle-biting dogs; well-trained dogs can be taught not to do undesirable things.

DID YOU KNOW?
The long-haired Chihuahua and the short-haired Chihuahua are classified as two separate breeds, even though both kinds can be found in a single litter of puppies.

Chihuahuas need a lot of attention and may get very annoyed if they get lonely. Some people buy more than one Chihuahua since they are such small animals. Chihuahuas usually get along well with other Chihuahuas. They may also get along with other small breeds, but it may not be a good idea to keep a Chihuahua with a much larger breed.

Chihuahuas make good watchdogs. They are very alert and very territorial. Size does not seem to matter to this tiny dog. The Chihuahua firmly stands its ground against any large dog. It will strongly defend its territory and its owner, barking feverishly at the first sign of intruders. But Chihuahuas do not make good guard dogs. They may be fearless, but they are really no match for a Great Dane or a Saint Bernard—or a burglar.

Chihuahuas are very sensitive animals. They seem to understand people's moods. They get excited when spoken to sweetly, but will appear very sad and miserable when spoken to harshly. They have even been known to shed tears, though what causes this is not known.

Chihuahuas are very active, excitable dogs, but they are not a good pet choice for very young children. They need to be handled gently and kept free from harm. However, Chihuahuas that are socialized with children will get along with them nicely. Children need to be taught how to handle these delicate dogs.

Chihuahuas are good pets for apartment dwellers. These little dogs should never be left outside during the winter or on cool days. They need warm temperatures and cannot handle the cold. Many Chihuahua owners keep their pets warm by dressing them in dog sweaters.

Chihuahuas live longer than any other dog breed—between 11 and 18 years—and some have been know to live into their twenties!

INTERNET RESOURCES

http://3lbdogs.com/gatehouse/index.html "Chihuahua Kingdom"

http://www.cis.ohio-state.edu/hypertext/fac/usenet/dogs-faq/breeds/chihuahuas/faq.html "Chihuahuas Breed - FAQ"

http://www.k9web.com/dog-faqs/breeds/chihuahuas.html "The Chihuahua FAQ" by Melinda Casino

http://www.petnet.com.au/dogs/D120.html "Chihuahua (Long Coat)," by Denise Humphries

CHINESE SHAR-PEI

FAST FACTS

Scientific name	*Canis familaris* in Family Canidae, Order Carnivora
Cost	Up to $1,000 for show quality
Food	Commercial dog food
Housing	Can be kept indoors freely if properly trained; or may be kept in a wire mesh cage or in an outdoor kennel. Outdoors, dog needs shelter. Indoors, dog needs a bed (or crate), and should have chew toys.
Training	Easy to train but needs firmness to keep from becoming too dominant. Can housebreak using a crate, or paper train; should learn to wear collar and leash; can learn basic commands, such as "Sit," "Come," "Stay," "Heel," and "No." May also learn tricks such as rolling over, playing dead, fetching.
Special notes	Before getting a shar-pei puppy, check with the breeder to make sure the parents do not have hip or knee defects, eye problems, or thyroid deficiency (which can cause skin problems). Have respiratory infections treated promptly. Some puppies need surgery on excess skin to prevent ulcers in eyes.

CHINESE SHAR-PEI

IF YOU HAD TO DESCRIBE a Chinese shar-pei in one word, you'd probably say "wrinkles!" It looks like it is wearing a plush fur coat that is too large for it, so that its loose skin forms rolls and folds and wrinkles all over its body and head. Shar-pei puppies are especially wrinkly. They usually lose many of their wrinkles as they grow up. This exotic dog breed is a relatively new addition to the American Kennel Club; in fact, no other breed has exploded so rapidly from the brink of extinction to huge popularity.

Pet owners say that shar-peis are very lovable animals. They are very smart, easy to train, and make excellent pets.

THE ORIGIN OF THE CHINESE SHAR-PEI

The Chinese shar-pei is an ancient breed, dating back about 2,000 years. It is believed to have originated during the Han Dynasty (206 B.C. to A.D. 220) in the small village of Tai Li in the southern Chinese province of Kwangtung. Statues from that time show a dog that looks very similar to the shar-pei. There is also a manuscript dating from the thirteenth century that describes a wrinkled dog with characteristics much like those of the shar-pei.

The early Chinese shar-pei dogs were used to hunt wild boar, guard people's homes, and protect livestock from predators. For centuries, these dogs were highly valued in China because of their strength and intelligence. These admirable traits prompted gamblers to use shar-peis as fighting dogs, but the dogs were not good fighters. Although their loose skin helped them to wriggle out of an opponent's grip, they were not as vicious as other fighting breeds, such as bulldogs and mastiffs. Their numbers were already declining when the Chinese Communists came into power after World War II. In 1947 the Chinese government placed a heavy tax on dogs, so that only the rich could afford to own one. Dog breeding was also banned. The government then ordered all dogs to be destroyed in a mass extermination program. By 1950, only scattered clusters of shar-peis were known to exist.

In 1973, Hong Kong dog breeder Matgo Law requested help from American dog lovers to "Save the Chinese shar-pei." The response was tremendous, but since the shar-pei was so rare, only a limited number of these dogs were sent to the United States. The new shar-pei owners formed their own shar-pei club and registry. The Chinese Shar-Pei Club of America had its first meeting in 1974. Interest in these unusual dogs increased rapidly, and the breed was finally recognized by the American Kennel Club in October 1991.

American breeders produced a dog that is very different from the ancient Chinese shar-pei. It has shorter legs, a stockier body, and a lot more wrinkles.

CHINESE SHAR-PEIS AS PETS

The Chinese shar-pei is a medium-size dog, standing 18 to 20 inches (46 to 51 centimeters) tall at the shoulders, and weighing an average 40 to 55 pounds (18 to 25 kilograms). The shar-pei has a hippopotamus-shaped muzzle and a characteristic blue-black tongue. The chow chow is the only other dog breed with a blue-black tongue, which is one of the main reasons scientists believe that the two may share a common ancestry.

The Chinese shar-pei's heavily wrinkled coat is very rough and coarse. In fact, the name *shar-pei* actually means "sand skin." The sandpaperlike coat is so harsh that it may irritate your skin if it touches you. The shar-pei's coat comes in a variety of solid colors including cream, black, apricot, chocolate, fawn, and red.

Shar-peis are natural watchdogs. They do not bark often but will let you know if a stranger approaches. Shar-peis form strong bonds with their owners and seldom wander away from their home. Owners must always be firm with their shar-

Leader of the Pack

Dogs, by nature, are pack animals. In the wild they live in small groups with a complex social structure. The members of the pack live and hunt together and may share in the care and feeding of the young. Every pack has a leader, called the alpha dog. The alpha dog is intelligent, able to lead the hunt, and provides protection for its members. The alpha dog is not vicious or aggressive, but is a strong, confident leader.

Dogs make good pets because they see their human owners as their pack and give them their loyalty and affection. Normally, a pet dog sees its main caretaker as the alpha dog. Sometimes, however, a Chinese shar-pei may try to take over the position of alpha dog in a human family. The owner must be firm to establish just who the "leader of the pack" is.

peis, though, because a shar-pei will become dominant and difficult to manage if it knows it can get away with things.

Shar-peis are highly intelligent. They are among the easiest dogs to housetrain, and they learn commands and tricks quickly. Shar-peis are very obedient, but they may get bored easily and will appear to be stubborn.

The Chinese shar-pei is not only a great conversation piece but is also a great companion. Its life span is 10 to 12 years.

> **DID YOU KNOW?**
> The shar-pei's pushed-in muzzle, which is shared by other dogs such as bulldogs and pugs, often causes snoring and snorting.

INTERNET RESOURCES

http://sunset.backbone.olemiss.edu/~lwaej/history.html "The Chinese Shar-Pei"

http://w3.mgr.com/mgr/howell/bobpages/breeds/chi_shar.htm "Chinese Shar-Pei"

http://www.barkbytes.com/history/chishar.htm "History of the Chinese Shar-Pei," by Lorraine Jones

http://www.driveninc.com/cruzzz/sharpei.htm "Choosing a Chinese Shar-Pei," by Tina Wissen

http://www.geocities.com/Heartland/Estates/7746/history.htm "History of the Chinese Shar-Pei"

http://www.k9web.com/dog-faqs/breeds/sharpeis.html "Chinese Shar-Pei," by Heidi Merkli

http://www.petsupport.com/DOGS/ALL/chinesesharpei.html "Chinese Shar-Pei" (PetSupport™ USA Canine Reference Library)

http://www.4shar-pei.com/cspfacts.htm "Facts About the Chinese Shar-Pei"

FAST FACTS

Scientific name	*Canis familaris* in Family Canidae, Order Carnivora
Cost	Up to $1,000 for show quality
Food	Commercial dog food
Housing	Can be kept indoors freely if properly trained; or may be kept in a wire mesh cage. Dog needs a bed (or crate) and chew toys. Generally not an outdoor dog; needs to be with its human family.
Training	A lot of patience needed for training. Dog treats are very effective for tricks. Can housebreak using a crate, or paper train; should learn to wear collar and leash; can learn basic commands, such as "Sit," "Come," "Stay," "Heel," and "No." May also learn tricks such as rolling over, playing dead, fetching.
Special notes	Relatively clean, non-smelly; needs moderate exercise. Back ailments (like a "slipped disc") are so common even in young dachshunds that catalogs sell special wheelchairs for them. They regard hamsters, rabbits, and other small pets as prey.

DACHSHUND

PEOPLE SOMETIMES CALL the dachshund a "wiener dog" or "hotdog." With its long, slender body and short legs, this dog does look a bit like a hotdog, especially as it is pictured in cartoons. But dachshunds were not bred hundreds of years ago to look funny. They were originally used as hunting dogs, the smallest dog breed ever used for hunting. They were bred to slip in and out of burrows to hunt their prey.

Today, dachshunds are kept mainly as pets. They form very close bonds with their owners, but they are quite independent and may be harder to train than other dogs.

THE ORIGIN OF THE DACHSHUND

Some researchers believe that the dachshund breed dates back thousands of years. There are carvings of dachshund-shaped dogs in ancient Egyptian tombs built about 1500 B.C. But there is no real evidence that they were the ancestors of the modern breed.

Scientists do know, however, that today's dachshund breed originated in Germany during the 1400s. For the next few centuries, these dogs were bred to hunt badgers. In fact, the name *dachshund* comes from German words meaning "badger dog." The badger-hunting dachshunds were strong, sturdy, courageous dogs. They could dig up the ground of a badger's burrow and use their long, slender bodies to slip into the tunnel and hold their own against the vicious attack of a

---

Branches on the Family Tree

It is thought that dachshunds may have been bred from basset hounds, which are also relatively long-bodied, short-legged dogs. (In French, basset *means "low-set.") Cardigan Welsh corgis—small, hardy dogs that were bred for farm work and herding cattle in Wales—are descended from the dachshund family.* Corgi *comes from either* cor *("dwarf") or* cur *("working dog").*

25- to 40-pound (11- to 18-kilogram) badger cornered in its den. Dachshunds also hunted rabbits, foxes, and even wild boar. The dogs would hunt in packs against wild boar, which are strong, fierce fighters.

Dachshunds were first brought to the United States in 1885. Over the next few decades, they grew in popularity. By 1913, dachshunds were among the ten best-represented breeds in dog shows. However, during World War I, the dachshund's popularity in America suffered because of the breed's German name and origin. After the war, a few U.S. breeders imported some dachshunds from Germany and built up the stock in America. Eventually, the dachshund started to grow in popularity once again. When World War II started, the American breeders were well established and dachshunds were too familiar and too popular to suffer from their long-ago link to the enemy.

> ## Breeding for Variety
>
> *The original dachshund was a medium-size dog with a smooth coat. It was probably bred with terrier stock to produce the wire-haired dachshunds, whose coats provided protection against burrs and thorns. Spaniels were probably used to produce the long-haired dachshunds, which were used as bird dogs. Smooth-coats still remain the most popular type of dachshund in the United States.*

DACHSHUNDS AS PETS

The dachshund is a short dog that stands low to the ground. The standard dachshund is 9 inches (23 centimeters) tall at the shoulders and weighs from 16 to 32 pounds (about 7 to 15 kilograms). The miniature dachshund stands only 5 to 6 inches (14 to 16 centimeters) tall and weighs an average of 11 pounds (5 kilograms).

The three coat types—smooth-coat, long-haired, and wire-haired—are all sturdy, active, and playful dogs. Some experts say there are differences in temperament depending on their coat type: Wire-haired dachshunds tend to be mischievous, for example, and the long-haired type more timid and gentle. Like people, however, individual dachshunds may also have different personalities depending on their heredity and experiences. They are generally friendly dogs and can be good with children if they are properly socialized as puppies.

Today's dachshund is no longer a hunter but still has hunting instincts. It may try to dig a tunnel under the covers in your bed or try to dig up the ground in the backyard. Originally bred as scent hounds, dachshunds are extremely sensitive to smells. They tend to follow an interesting scent quite single-mindedly and can never be trusted off the leash anywhere that there is a chance of their getting into street or highway traffic.

Dachshunds are very affectionate dogs, but at the same time they are very independent. (This trait comes from their background as hunting dogs that could find and catch prey on their own.) Their independence makes training rather difficult. In fact, it is not uncommon to hear an owner say, "My dachshund is housebroken most of the time." If they don't feel like going outside or the weather is bad, they may think it's okay to relieve themselves inside the house. Dachshunds are smart and will test you. They will jump on the furniture even after they are told "No!" fifty times. Training is very important, though. Like all dogs, dachshunds need to learn the basic commands, and owners should be patient, firm, and consistent.

> **DID YOU KNOW?**
> Dachshunds are very playful animals, but they should not be allowed to jump from heights. Such a jump can hurt a dachshund, causing serious and long-lasting back problems.

Dachshunds are very alert and protective dogs, which makes them good watchdogs. They are quick to bark when a stranger approaches. But they can be rather noisy at times.

Dachshunds may not be for everyone. But if this dog sounds interesting to you, be aware that the breed is more strong-willed than other dogs and may require a lot of patience. The dachshund has a long life span, as many as 12 to 16 years.

INTERNET RESOURCES

http://w3.mgr.com/mgr/howell/bobpages/breeds/dachshun.htm "Dachshund"

http://www.canismajor.com/dog/dachs.html "Dog Owner's Guide Profile: The Dachshund," by Norma Bennett Woolf

http://www.cis.ohio-state.edu/hypertext/...enet/dogs-faq/breeds/dachshunds/faq.html "Dachshund Breed-FAQ," by Steven Michelson

http://www.digitaldog.com/dachshund.html "Dachshund in Brief"

http://www.petnet.com.au/dogs/D126.html "Dachshund (Miniature Long-Haired)" and http://www.petnet.com.au/dogs/D128.html "Dachshund (Smooth-Haired)," by Denise Humphries

FAST FACTS

Scientific name	*Canis familaris* in Family Canidae, Order Carnivora
Cost	Adoption fee usually $75 to $225
Food	Commercial dog food
Housing	Can be kept indoors freely if properly trained; or may be kept in a wire mesh cage. Needs a soft bed. Cannot stay outdoors in cold weather.
Training	Needs a lot of patience for training. Dog treats are very effective for tricks. Can housebreak using a crate or paper train; should learn to wear collar and leash; can learn basic commands, such as "Sit," "Come," "Stay," "Heel," "Down," and "No." May also learn tricks such as rolling over, playing dead; may not be willing to fetch.
Special notes	Needs plenty of attention and exercise. If allowed outside in a yard, must be securely fenced; *a chain run is dangerous*.

GREYHOUND

FOR CENTURIES, GREYHOUNDS have been used as racing animals. In fact, they have been bred for their speed, making them the fastest dogs in the world. Greyhounds are admired for their racing background, but these animals can make great pets, too.

When greyhounds retire from racing, families can adopt these dogs as pets. Greyhounds are remarkable animals. Outdoors, it is an amazing sight to watch them run with such tremendous energy. But indoors, they become quiet and affectionate and fit perfectly into the family. They may even become regular "couch potatoes." A retired greyhound does not take long to adjust in a new home.

THE ORIGIN OF THE GREYHOUND

The greyhound is one of the oldest of dog breeds. It originated in ancient Egypt as early as 6,000 years ago. Carvings of these dogs appeared on the walls of Egyptian tombs. They were even mummified, and the death of a greyhound rated second in importance to the death of a son. In addition to being highly valued companions, greyhounds were also used for hunting. They were so fast they could easily catch game such as rabbits or even gazelles. Greyhounds belong to a group called sighthounds. They hunt by sight rather than scent.

In ancient Greece the greyhound became a favorite among the royal families. Many Greek vases had pictures of greyhounds on them. In the second century, coursing became popular. In this ancient sport, greyhounds would chase a live hare around a track. The dogs were judged for their speed and agility.

From Greece, greyhounds were taken to ancient Rome. They were owned by the nobility; in the Roman empire peasants who owned greyhounds were seriously punished. Roman soldiers often took greyhounds with them on campaigns

> **DID YOU KNOW?**
> The greyhound can run up to 40 miles (64 kilometers) per hour or more, making it the second fastest land animal on earth; only the cheetah is faster.

in other countries. Through their travels, the greyhound spread to France, Great Britain, and Ireland.

The greyhound was first brought to America during the 1500s by Spanish explorers. But large numbers of greyhounds did not appear until the 1800s, when many people from Ireland and Britain started settling in the midwestern and western United States. Greyhounds were often let loose in the open fields to hunt rabbits that might destroy the settlers' crops.

The European settlers brought their love of the sport of coursing with them, but many people were too upset by the bloodiness of the sport to watch the greyhounds kill rabbits. In 1912 an artificial lure was invented, and soon greyhound racing grew in popularity. Since greyhounds hunt by sight rather than scent, using a "fake" rabbit was not a problem. The use of an artificial lure brought major changes to the sport of greyhound racing. Greyhounds were no longer a dog breed of nobility. Anyone could own them.

Greyhound racing continues to be a popular sport in parts of the United States, as well as in many other countries. Animal activists are against greyhound racing because greyhounds must retire at the age of only 3 or 4 years, when their bodies start to slow down. Unfortunately, thousands of greyhounds too old to race (as well as those that are not fast enough) are destroyed each year. Within the past decade or so, however, organizations have been formed to promote the adoption of retired racing greyhounds. Since these programs began, many people have discovered that greyhounds make really great pets.

GREYHOUNDS AS PETS

The greyhound is a slender, sleek-looking dog. It stands 25 to 27 inches (64 to 69 centimeters) tall at the shoulder and weighs 60 to 70 pounds (27 to 32 kilograms).

Greyhounds are very gentle and sweet-natured. They are very patient with children. Some dogs may growl or snap at a child when they become annoyed, but greyhounds are more likely to walk away from the situation than act out.

Greyhounds have an easygoing temperament. If you want to play, the greyhound will be more than happy to play. But if you want to sit around and watch television, the greyhound will be happy to do that, too. (Ex-racers are used to long periods of rest between short bursts of intense exercise during a race.) Since greyhounds are born racers, they do need exercise. They should be walked about three to four times a week. Greyhounds must be trained to use a leash because they will instinctively run off.

DID YOU KNOW?

Greyhounds are not outdoor dogs. For thousands of years, greyhounds have been kept in the homes of their masters. They seem to love people and want to be close to them.

Miniature Greyhounds

How would you like a dog that looks like a greyhound, but is much smaller? The whippet belongs to the same group of dogs as the greyhound, the sighthounds. The whippet stands 17 to 20 inches (43 to 51 centimeters) tall at the shoulders and weighs only 27 to 30 pounds (12.5 to 13.5 kilograms). Like the greyhound, the whippet is a speedy racing dog. The whippet was originally created by crossing greyhounds with several other dog breeds, including a small greyhound called the Italian greyhound and a now-extinct long-legged terrier. The whippet's small size made it cheaper to feed and house than the greyhound.

Today, whippets and Italian greyhounds are sold as pets. The Italian greyhound is even smaller than the whippet, standing only 6 to 10 inches (15 to 25 centimeters) tall at the shoulders and weighing 7 to 10 pounds (3 to 4.5 kilograms). These miniature greyhounds are fascinating dogs—adorable, gentle, and devoted to their owners.

Greyhounds are generally healthy dogs and when properly cared for, they have a life span of 12 to 14 years.

INTERNET RESOURCES

http://nga.jc.net/faq.htm "Greyhounds, Frequently Asked Questions"

http://w3.mgr.com/mgr/howell/bobpages/breeds/greyhoun.htm "Greyhound"

http://www.adopt-a-greyhound.org/ "The Greyhound Project" (information on greyhounds, adoption, and a worldwide list of agencies and contacts)

http://www.eskimo.com/~kstevens/gpa "Greyhounds Make Great Pets!"

http://www.greyhounds2.org/ "Adopt a Greyhound Atlanta, Inc."

http://www.seabrookgreyhoundpark.com/adopt.htm "Seabrook Greyhound Park: Greyhound Adoption"

http://www.usadog.org/docs/faq.html "USA Defenders of Greyhounds FAQ"

FAST FACTS

Scientific name	*Canis familaris* in Family Canidae, Order Carnivora
Cost	Up to $1,000 for show quality
Food	Commercial dog food
Housing	Can be kept indoors freely if properly trained; or may be kept in a wire mesh cage or in an outdoor kennel. Outdoors, dog needs shelter. Indoors, dog needs a bed (or crate) and should have chew toys.
Training	Easy to train, but start early. Use positive rewards and enthusiastic praise. Can housebreak using a crate, or paper train; should learn to wear collar and leash; can learn basic commands, such as "Sit," "Come," "Stay," "Heel," and "No." May also learn tricks such as rolling over, playing dead, fetching, carrying newspaper, and pulling a wagon.
Special notes	Check with breeder about hereditary conditions such as heart disease in the parents; other serious health problems common in the breed are bloat, cancer, and epilepsy.

SAINT BERNARD

FOR HUNDREDS OF YEARS, Saint Bernards have been known and admired for their bravery in rescuing thousands of people from the treacherous snow-covered mountains of the Swiss Alps. Their historic efforts have made them one of the most remarkable dogs in the world.

The Saint Bernard is a massive dog whose size may appear frightening to some people. But this dog is really a gentle giant. Saint Bernards love people and are very willing to please their owners. They are not for everyone, though. Their huge size makes them an enormous responsibility. They eat more, make bigger messes, and need more attention and training than smaller dog breeds.

THE ORIGIN OF THE SAINT BERNARD

The Saint Bernard is a very ancient breed. It is believed that these dogs were first brought to Switzerland by invading Roman armies during the second and third centuries. These dogs were used in valley farms and Alpine dairies for a variety of purposes—guarding flocks, herding livestock, pulling carts—as well as for companionship.

In 1050 a monk known as Saint Bernard of Menthon founded a monastery high in the Swiss Alps, on a road later named the Great Saint Bernard Pass. This mountain road, which connected Switzerland and Italy, was covered with as much as 32 feet (nearly 10 meters) of snow much of the year. Some of the monks served as guides for travelers and provided them with food and shelter. Sometimes the monks had to rescue people from the dangerous snow-covered mountains.

It is believed that dogs were first brought to the Saint Bernard Hospice in the mid-1600s by monks who had been visiting the valley. These "valley dogs" served as watchdogs for the hospice and companions for the monks during the long, lonely winter months.

The monks most likely took their dogs along with them on rescues. They soon noticed that the dogs were great pathfinders in the snowy mountains, and their amazing sense of smell could locate people in snowstorms. They could even find a person buried under piles of snow and could somehow sense when an avalanche was going to occur.

By the early 1700s the Saint Bernard, as the dogs were later called, were well known for rescuing travelers lost in the snow. The monks bred these dogs at the monastery from giant mastiff stock and raised them to be strong and dependable. When Saint Bernards found someone in the snow, they would lie down next to the person to provide body warmth. If a victim was unconscious, the dogs would lick the person's face, and one of them would rush back to the monastery to get help.

The first Saint Bernards had short coats. But in 1830 the monks decided to breed the Saint Bernard with the Newfoundland, a long-haired dog. They hoped that the cross would give Saint Bernards a long coat to keep them warm in the bitter cold winters. Unfortunately, snow and ice built up in the long fur until it was so heavy the dogs could not move. So the monks stopped breeding long-haired dogs and gave all the long-haired puppies away to the people in nearby farms and towns. These dogs were bred with other long-haired dogs in the town. Since then, there have been short-haired and long-haired varieties of the Saint Bernard.

In the 1850s, Heinrich Schumacher became the first breeder to breed Saint Bernards outside the monastery. He was given some stock by the monks, and descendants of the monastery dogs were eventually sent to England, Russia, and the United States. By 1885 the Saint Bernard was registered with the American Kennel Club. The Saint Bernard Club of America was established in 1888, making it one of the oldest dog clubs in the country.

SAINT BERNARDS AS PETS

Saint Bernards are very large dogs. They have a strong, massive head and a tremendous body. Males are generally larger than females, standing 27.5 to 35.5

Barry the Saint Bernard

A dog named Barry, born in 1800, became the most famous Saint Bernard in history. During the twelve years of his service with the monastery, Barry saved forty lives. It was believed that Barry was killed during his forty-first rescue, but this was not true. Barry actually retired when he was 12 years old and died of old age two years later.

There is a monument to Barry in Paris, France, as a tribute to heroic dogs from the Saint Bernard monastery. People can now travel through the Alps in trains and cars, and dog rescues are no longer needed. (The last one was in 1897.) But the monks still breed Saint Bernards at their monastery and always keep a dog named Barry in memory of the canine hero.

inches (70 to 90 centimeters) at the shoulders, compared to 25.5 to 31.5 inches (65 to 80 centimeters) for females. Saint Bernards may weigh between 120 and 200 pounds (54 to 90 kilograms), males weighing more than females. The largest Saint Bernard on record was 310 pounds (140 kilograms)!

Saint Bernards may have a short or long coat. The coat is usually white, covered with patches that range from light golden brown to deep reddish brown. Often they also have a dark face mask.

Due to the Saint Bernard's large size, puppies need to be trained as early as possible. It is not very cute when the puppy grows into a 200-pound adult capable of destroying your house or unintentionally harming someone with its massive body. Saint Bernards are usually easy to train because they are eager to please their owners.

Saint Bernards seem to love children and have been known to be great babysitters. But they may accidentally harm young children because of their large size. A quick swat of the tail or a bump by their massive body could knock a child down to the ground. So children should not be left alone with Saint Bernards.

Saint Bernards make good watchdogs and will bark at the first sign of strangers. But they are too friendly to be guard dogs.

Saint Bernards are sweet, lovable animals that need a lot of attention and a lot of hard work. Owning a Saint Bernard can be very challenging, yet very rewarding. Unfortunately, as with other large dog breeds, the Saint Bernard has a short life span of 7 to 12 years.

DID YOU KNOW?

The Saint Bernard of the 1800s was much smaller than the Saint Bernard of the 1990s. Barry stood less than 26 inches (66 centimeters) at the shoulders, compared to more than 30 inches (76 centimeters) for a male Saint Bernard today.

DID YOU KNOW?

Saint Bernard puppies grow at an amazing rate. Puppies weigh about 1.5 pounds (less than 1 kilogram) at birth. During the first year, they gain about 3 pounds (almost 1.5 kilograms) each *week*. In three years, a puppy will grow to 100 times its birth weight!

INTERNET RESOURCES

http://w3.mgr.com/mgr/howell/bobpages/breeds/saint.htm "Saint Bernard"

http://www.akc.org/clubs/saints/fact.fiction.htm "Saint Bernard Club of America FACT AND FICTION: About Our Breed," by Arthur Hesser

http://www.akc.org/clubs/saints/info.packet.htm#questions "Saint Bernard Club of America Information Packet"

http://www.canismajor.com/dog/stbernrd.html "Dog Owner's Guide Profile: The St. Bernard," by Norma Bennett Woolf

http://www.digitaldog.com/saintbernardbrief.html "Saint Bernard in Brief"

http://www.k9web.com/dog-faqs/breeds/stbernard.html "Saint Bernards," by Cindy Tittle Moore

SHIH TZU

FAST FACTS

Scientific name	*Canis familaris* in Family Canidae, Order Carnivora
Cost	Up to $1,000 for show quality
Food	Commercial dog food
Housing	Can be kept indoors freely if properly trained; or may be kept in a wire mesh cage. Needs a bed (or crate) and chew toys. Should never be left outdoors for long periods of time.
Training	Needs a lot of patience for training. Dog treats are very effective for tricks. Can housebreak using a crate, or paper train; should learn to wear collar and leash; can learn basic commands, such as "Sit," "Come," "Stay," "Heel," and "No." May also learn tricks such as rolling over, playing dead, fetching, carrying newspaper.
Special notes	Before getting a shih tzu, ask about hereditary kidney disease; watch out for skin problems and allergies.

SHIH TZU

FOR THOUSANDS OF YEARS, shih tzus were kept as companions for Chinese royalty. They were highly valued members of the court, treated as well as the royal families. Today's shih tzu has traces of this aristocratic dog. It is an elegant-looking dog with a long, flowing coat, and it walks with confidence, almost arrogance.

Though shih tzus love to be catered to, they are not snobbish. These dogs are very friendly and sweet, and they get along well with people. They make great lapdogs and enjoy being close to their owners.

THE ORIGIN OF THE SHIH TZU

The shih tzu is one of the oldest dog breeds. Paintings and documents dated A.D. 624 indicate that a pair of shih tzus was brought to the Chinese court

> **DID YOU KNOW?**
> *Shih tzu* (pronounced "sheed zoo") means "lion dog." But this little dog doesn't hunt lions. The shih tzu got its name because it looks like a lion as depicted in traditional Oriental art.

from the Byzantine empire. Other legends suggest that the shih tzu originated in Tibet. In the seventeenth century, during the Manchu Dynasty, it was customary for the Dalai Lama of Tibet to send a pair of dogs as presents to the emperor of China. The shih tzu was a favorite of the Chinese royal family, and certain members of the court competed to breed varieties of the dog that would please the emperor. These dogs became a cross between the Lhasa apso and the Pekingese.

The shih tzus were treated as royalty. They stayed in the palace, slept on the royal silk sheets, ate from the emperor's personal table, and were protected by the palace guards, as well as by the Chinese army.

During the Chinese revolution in 1911, many shih tzus were destroyed because they were seen as a symbol of imperial rule. The breed was brought close to extinction. Fortunately, some of the dogs were saved and bred. Eventually, these palace dogs were sold to wealthy Chinese and to foreigners, as well.

Around 1930, Lady Brownrigg, an Englishwoman living in China, admired the shih tzu dogs she was lucky to see, and had the first pair sent to England. These dogs, along with a few shih tzus that were sent by an English officer on duty in China, became the stock that started the shih tzu's breeding history in England. Eventually, shih tzus were sent from England to the Scandinavian countries, to other countries in Europe, and to Australia. Shih tzus did not reach the United States until after World War II, when American soldiers stationed in England brought some of these exotic little dogs back with them when they returned to the States.

It was not until the 1960s that the shih tzu started to become popular among Americans. In 1969 the shih tzu was recognized by the American Kennel Club in the Toy Group.

SHIH TZUS AS PETS

The shih tzu is a small dog, standing 8 to 11 inches (20 to 28 centimeters) tall at the shoulders, and weighing 9 to 16 pounds (4.1 to 7.3 kilograms). The shih tzu is well known for its long, thick, luxurious coat. The coat is double-layered.

The underlayer helps to give the shih tzu an overall graceful appearance. The coat must be groomed regularly to avoid becoming tangled and matted. The coat comes in a wide variety of colors and patterns including black, black and white, gray and white, red and white, or gold.

The shih tzu makes a good watchdog. It will bark at the first sign of a stranger, but it does not yap, as some other toy breeds do. The shih tzu is very friendly and thrives on companionship, so strangers may not be strangers for long. The shih tzu may seek out the warm lap of a new "friend."

Shih tzus love people, but they may not be good pets for young children. They may not be able to handle a child's high activity level. They may feel threatened and become annoyed.

Shih tzus are very intelligent, but they are not as easy to train as some other dog breeds. With plenty of patience, shih tzus can be taught to follow commands and perform tricks.

The shih tzus' easygoing personality and friendly nature make them great companions. They have a life span of 12 to 14 years.

INTERNET RESOURCES

http://w3.mgr.com/mgr/howell/bobpages/breeds/shih_tzu.htm "Shih Tzu"

http://www.akc.org/shihtzu.htm "Shih Tzu—AKC Breed Standard"

http://www.canine-connections.com/features/may/character.htm "Shih Tzu Characteristics"

http://www.cheta.net/connect2/tarahaus/history.htm "Shih Tzu History"

http://www.k9web.com/dog-faqs/breeds/shih-tzus.html "Shih-Tzus," by Ruth A. Grimaldi

http://www.petnet.com.au/dogs/D173.html "Shih Tzu," by Denise Humphries

http://www.shihtzu.org/stinfo/astchist/astchist1/ "A Brief History of the Shih Tzu," by Victor Joris

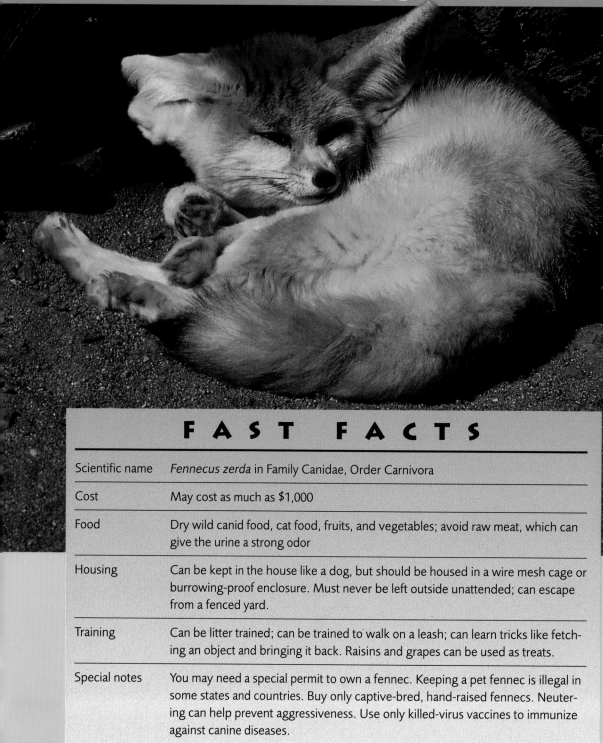

FAST FACTS

Scientific name	*Fennecus zerda* in Family Canidae, Order Carnivora
Cost	May cost as much as $1,000
Food	Dry wild canid food, cat food, fruits, and vegetables; avoid raw meat, which can give the urine a strong odor
Housing	Can be kept in the house like a dog, but should be housed in a wire mesh cage or burrowing-proof enclosure. Must never be left outside unattended; can escape from a fenced yard.
Training	Can be litter trained; can be trained to walk on a leash; can learn tricks like fetching an object and bringing it back. Raisins and grapes can be used as treats.
Special notes	You may need a special permit to own a fennec. Keeping a pet fennec is illegal in some states and countries. Buy only captive-bred, hand-raised fennecs. Neutering can help prevent aggressiveness. Use only killed-virus vaccines to immunize against canine diseases.

FENNEC

WE ALL KNOW THAT dogs make wonderful pets. But there's another member of the dog family that also makes a great pet—the fennec fox. Yes, a fox, but not the red or gray foxes that you may see running around your neighborhood. The fennec is an exotic fox that some people keep as a pet—just like you would keep a little pet dog.

Like dogs, the fennec, also called fennec fox, is a very affectionate and loyal companion. Owning a fennec fox is a unique experience and an enjoyable one, too. As with any pet, though, it needs proper care and plenty of attention.

THE BIG-EARED FOX

The fennec is easy to recognize—it's a fox with great big ears. The fennec fox is a very small animal, so its large ears are really noticeable. The fennec's ears are perfectly adapted to the environment in which it lives.

The fennec fox lives in the dry, hot desert. Its ears help to protect it from the hot desert sun. The fennec's big ears work like a radiator—they give off excess body heat to keep the fennec's body cool.

The fennec's ears also act as antennas and pick up even the slightest sounds. These little foxes depend on their keen hearing to hunt down prey and to avoid predators.

DID YOU KNOW?
Dogs cool down by panting; people cool down by sweating. But both dogs and people lose water from their bodies when they do this. Living in the desert, the fennec has to conserve water, and no water is wasted when its ears give off heat to cool down its body.

THE LIFE OF A FENNEC FOX

In the wild the fennec fox can be found in the Sahara Desert in North Africa, and in the Arabian and Sinai peninsulas. Fennecs live in deep underground burrows for protection from the hot sun. The burrow may turn into a series of tunnels, which lead to storage chambers and a maternal den. The burrows may be as much as 33 feet (10 meters) deep.

Fennecs are very fast diggers. They are so fast that they seem to "sink" into the sand. This really helps when they are trying to catch prey or escape predators. Like many other desert animals, fennecs rest in their cool underground burrows during the daytime and come out at night to hunt. They may stock up on food by storing it in their burrows. Since the desert is so dry, they can go for long periods without water, but they will drink if water is available.

The fennec fox is the smallest member of the dog family. Its body is about 14 to 16 inches (36 to 41 centimeters) long, with an 8-inch (20-centimeter) bushy tail and 6-inch (15-centimeter) ears. It weighs only 2 to 3 pounds (0.9 to 1.4 kilograms). The fennec's sandy-colored fur is thick and silky. Desert animals do not usually have thick fur. But the fennec's thick fur helps to insulate the fox from colder nights as well as the daytime heat. The light color also reflects heat, which helps the animal stay cool. The fennec's feet are heavily furred to protect it from the hot sand, and the extra padding helps it run quickly across loose sand without sinking.

Fennecs may live in family groups, alone, or in pairs. After mating, an adult male and female stay together until the young grow up. The male will defend the young even though he is not allowed in the mother's den.

Fennecs communicate with one another with growls, yelps, and short yapping barks. They may also communicate through scent-marking. The males urinate on certain spots to tell foxes in the area that another fox is nearby.

FENNEC FOX PETS

The fennec fox is the most social of all of the foxes. That is one of the reasons why they can be kept as pets. Fennecs can be easily tamed. When they are hand-raised, they become gentle and lovable, but fennecs that are raised by their mother are not as friendly.

Stock Up on Band-Aids!

Your friendly fennec fox may give you a few little nips with its needle-sharp teeth. It's not being bad-tempered or aggressive, just playing the way it would with another fox. Lightly squeezing its muzzle when it nips can help to discourage this behavior, which is usually outgrown by four or five months of age.

Fennecs can be treated as you would a pet dog. They can be just as affectionate and loyal as any dog. They will sleep on your lap while you watch television and snuggle with you under the covers at bedtime.

Many fennecs can learn how to use a litter box like a cat. They can also be taught tricks, like fetching objects and bringing them back to you. Play sessions with toys to chase and retrieve can help work off some of these active little animals' excess energy and keep them from getting bored.

A pet fennec fox should be taught to walk on a leash and should never be taken outside without it except for supervised play sessions in a securely fenced-in yard. Otherwise, its natural instincts will take over. The need to hunt and explore is very powerful. If a quick-moving grasshopper or butterfly catches its attention, your pet fennec will take off in pursuit and may quickly get lost.

Like many dogs, the fennec fox has a life span of 10 to 12 years.

INTERNET RESOURCES

http://aztec.asu.edu/phxzoo/foxfenec.html "Fennec Fox" (Phoenix Zoo)

http://sazoo-aq.org/fennec.htm "Fennec Fox" (San Antonio Zoo)

http://www.birminghamzoo.com/ao/mammal/fennicfx.htm "Fennec Fox"

http://www.blarg.net/~critter/articles/canines/fennec1.html "Fennec Fox," by Roger Dingman

http://www.blarg.net/~critter/articles/canines/fennec3.html "Keeping Fennec Foxes," by Lynn Hill

http://www.geocities.com/Heartland/4075/fox.html "The Desert Fox," by Donna Maria Waltz (with lots of photos)

http://www.geocities.com/RainForest/4707/Fennec.htm "Fennec Fox"

http://www.livingdesert.org/wildlife/animals/fennec_fox.htm "Fennec Fox"

http://www.lpzoo.com/animals/mammals/facts/fennec_fox.html "Species Data Sheet ** Fennec Fox" (Lincoln Park Zoo)

http://www.phillyzoo.org/pz0041.htm "Fennec Fox" (Philadelphia Zoo)

http://www.rzu2u.com/fennec.htm "The Fennec Fox," by Pat Storey

NOT A PET!

IN JAPAN, AKITAS OFTEN serve as the family's trusted baby-sitter. And yet, some years ago an Akita in New Jersey was sentenced to be destroyed after it severely injured a neighbor's child. (The dog eventually received a special pardon from the governor, on condition that it would go to a family without children and would be exiled from the state of New Jersey forever.) Meanwhile, a series of letters in the popular Ann Landers newspaper column claimed that chows were particularly likely to be involved in dogbite cases; and there have been so many attacks on people by pit bulls that it is illegal to own them in some communities. (Defenders of the breed claim that pit bulls are not really vicious unless they have been trained as attack dogs.)

Dogs have been trusted companions of people for thousands of years. But some experts believe that there are some breeds of dogs that should not be kept as pets. They say that in some cases breeders have put too much emphasis on a dog's appearance rather than its temperament, and serious hereditary health problems have been reinforced by inbreeding until they have become all too common in certain breeds.

In this book we have tried to give you an idea of what to expect—both good and bad—from a few interesting breeds. However, although a person buying a purebred puppy can predict to some degree what it will look like and how it will act when it grows up, there is a lot of individual variation. A purebred dog that does not meet the standards for dog shows may make a fine family pet. (It will also cost considerably less, and purebred dogs may even be found in an animal shelter.) A mixed-breed "mutt" can also turn out to be a friendly, happy, and healthy family pet.

Knowing what to expect is important when you are planning to take on the responsibilities of pet ownership. A particular breed may be perfect for some people but not for you. The result of a mismatch may be a disaster. Sadly, nearly half of all puppies do not last a year with the people who adopted them as pets. They may be returned to the breeders, left at a shelter, put to death, or just abandoned to the miserable life of a stray on the streets.

DID YOU KNOW?

Registration papers issued by the AKC or another dog club are no guarantee that a purebred dog will have all the characteristics of its breed, or that it will be healthy. They just show that its parents were both members of a recognized breed.

Many problems can be avoided by getting a purebred dog from a reputable breeder who selects the parents carefully and gives the puppies plenty of loving attention early in their lives. Animal rescue organizations also have devoted volunteers who work hard to socialize the animals in shelters and try to match them to people who will give them the best home.

FOR FURTHER INFORMATION

Note: Before attempting to keep a kind of pet that is new to you, it is a good idea to read one or more pet manuals about that species or breed. Check your local library, pet shop, or bookstore. Search for information on the species or breed on the Internet.

BOOKS

American Kennel Club. *The Complete Dog Book*, 19th edition. New York: Howell Book House, 1997.

American Kennel Club. *The Complete Dog Book for Kids.* New York: Howell Book House, 1996.

Coile, Caroline D. *Encyclopedia of Dog Breeds.* New York: Barron's Educational Series, 1998.

Fogle, Bruce. *Encyclopedia of the Dog.* New York: Dorling-Kindersley, 1995.

Walkowicz, Chris. *The Perfect Match.* New York: Macmillan, 1996.

PERIODICALS

AKC Gazette - The Official Journal for the Sport of Purebred Dogs (a monthly magazine published by the American Kennel Club). Reprints of articles and subscription information can be found at their Web site: **http://www.akc.org/ gazet.htm**

Dog Owner's Guide (a bimonthly magazine for pet and show dog owners). Reprints of articles and subscription information can be found at their Web site: **http://www.canis-major.com/dog/guide.html**

Dog World (a monthly magazine for dog lovers). Reprints and subscription information at their Web site: **http://www.dogworldmag.com/**

Hoflin Dog Magazines (magazines on individual breeds). Subscription information at their Web site: **http://www.hoflin.com/Magazines/Magazines.html**

List of print magazines on dogs at **http://www.rapidnet.com/~cldavies/dogs.html**

INTERNET RESOURCES

http://www.akc.org/breeds.htm "AKC Breeds" (how to choose the right breed for you and other questions to consider about dog ownership)

http://www.animalsforsale.com/exotic.htm "The Joy and the Commitment," by Pat Storer (things to consider about owning exotic pets)

http://www.nwlink.com/~pawprint/petparts_b4ubuy.html "Before You Buy" (things to consider before getting a pet)

http://www.petz.com/ PF Magic offers software for "virtual" dogs and cats that you raise and care for on your computer. With the *Dogz* 3 CD-ROM you can "adopt" dogs of various breeds, feed them, breed them, and let them play among the Windows while you work. The Web site provides demos, ordering information, links to Internet pet sites, and bulletin boards for Petz owners to exchange information and post pictures.

INDEX

Page numbers in *italics* refer to illustrations.